THE GOD IN YOU BIBLE STUDY SERIES

JESUS!
GOD IN YOU
MADE POSSIBLE

A Bible Study by

Churches Alive!

MINISTERING TO THE CHURCHES OF THE WORLD
600 Meridian Avenue, Suite 200
San Jose, California 95126-3427

Published by

NAVPRESS
BRINGING TRUTH TO LIFE
NavPress Publishing Group
P.O. Box 35001, Colorado Springs, Colorado 80935

OUR GUARANTEE TO YOU

We believe so strongly in the message of our books that we are making this quality guarantee to you. If for any reason you are disappointed with the content of this book, return the title page to us with your name and address and we will refund to you the list price of the book. To help us serve you better, please briefly describe why you were disappointed. Mail your refund request to: NavPress, P.O. Box 35002, Colorado Springs, CO 80935.

ISBN 08910-90924

Cover Illustration: Catherine Kanner

Scripture quotations are from the *Holy Bible: New International Version*
(NIV). Copyright © 1973, 1978, 1984, International Bible Society. Used
by permission of Zondervan Bible Publishers.

Printed in the United States of America

14 15 16 17 18 19 20/05 04 03 02 01 00 99

*Because we share kindred aims for helping local churches fulfill
Christ's Great Commission to "go and make disciples," NavPress and
Churches Alive have joined efforts on certain strategic publishing
projects that are intended to bring effective disciplemaking resources
into the service of the local church.*

*For more than a decade, Churches Alive has teamed up wtth churches
of all denominations to establish vigorous disciplemaking ministries.
At the same time. NavPress has focused on publishing Bible studies,
books, and other resources that have grown out of The Navigators'
fifty years of disciplemaking experience.*

*Now, together, we're working to offer special products like this one
that are designed to stimulate a deeper, more fruitful commitment to
Christ in the local gatherings of His Church.*

*The GOD IN YOU BIBLE Bible Study Series was written by Russ
Korth, Ron Wormser, Jr., and Ron Wormser, Sr., of Churches Alive.
Many individuals from both Churches Alive and NavPress con-
tributed greatly in bringing this project to publication.*

Contents

About the Author

In your hand you have just one item of a *wide range* of discipling helps, authored and developed by Churches Alive with *one overall, church-centered, biblical concept* in mind: GROWING BY DISCIPLING!

Convinced that the local church is the heart of God's plan for the world, a number of Christian leaders joined in 1973 to form Churches Alive. They saw the need for someone to work hand-in-hand with local churches to help them develop fruitful discipleship ministries.

Today, the ministry of Churches Alive has grown to include personal consulting assistance to church leaders, a variety of discipleship books and materials, and training conferences for clergy and laypeople. These methods and materials have proven effective in churches large and small of over forty-five denominations.

From their commitment and experience in church ministry, Churches Alive developed the Growing by Discipling plan to help you

- minister to people at their levels of maturity.
- equip people for ministry.
- generate mature leaders.
- perpetuate quality.
- balance growth and outreach.

Every part of Growing by Discipling works together in harmony to meet the diverse needs of people—from veteran church members to the newly awakened in Christ. This discipling approach allows you to integrate present fruitful ministries and create additional ones through the new leaders you develop.

This concept follows Christ's disciplemaking example by helping you to meet people at their points of need. Then, you help them build their dependence on God so they experience His love and power. Finally, you equip them to reach out to others in a loving, effective, and balanced ministry of evangelism and helping hands.

Headquartered in San Jose, California, with staff across the United States and in Europe, Churches Alive continues to expand its Ministry in North America and overseas.

Introduction

Jesus Christ is the center of Christianity. He is the Author, the Sustainer, the Finisher, the Foundation, the Head, the Beginning, and the End. He is all in all.

Jesus claimed to be the door through which you can enter into a relationship with God, a relationship so close that God takes residence in you.

To understand Jesus, the One who makes God in you possible, you will study His birth, His life, and His death.

HIS BIRTH (chapters 1-2). No other person entered the world as uniquely and significantly as Jesus. You will look at Jesus' birth from both the earthly and heavenly perspectives.

HIS LIFE (chapters 3-7). The life of Jesus reveals who He is. You will examine five interesting and important facets to his character.

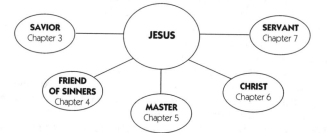

HIS DEATH (chapters 8-12). Almost half of the content of the four Gospels (Matthew, Mark, Luke, and John) is concerned with events surrounding the death of Jesus. It is through His execution and subsequent resurrection that Jesus completed His greatest work. You will study two of the most important events of the week before His death—the Last Supper and His prayer just before He was arrested; then His death, burial, resurrection, and ascension.

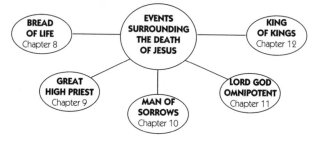

HOW TO USE THIS BIBLE STUDY. This book leads you through a unique approach to making the Bible meaningful. In each chapter you will study one passage, not isolated verses, to explore some of the major themes of God's Word. In the process, you'll learn Bible study methods that will be useful for the rest of your life.

You will gain maximum benefit from this book by completing the questions about the study passage and then meeting with a group of people to discuss what you discovered in your study.

No doubt, your group could spend many weeks exploring the richness of just one of these Bible passages. But much greater profit accompanies a pace of one chapter each week. This stride guarantees sustained enthusiasm that will leave people wanting more.

The leader's guide designed for this series aids the group leader in launching and guiding the discussion. It provides help for using the series in a home-study group or a classroom setting.

HINTS TO ENHANCE YOUR EXPERIENCE. The translation used in writing this study is the *New International Version* (NIV) of the Bible. All quotations are from this translation.

Though written using the NIV, this workbook adapts readily to other Bible translations. In fact, it adds interest and variety in group discussions when people use different translations.

Your book includes space to answer each question. But some people choose to mark some of their answers in an inexpensive Bible. Creating a study Bible like this allows a person to benefit from notes and information year after year.

Above all, *use* the insight you gain. The truths of the Bible were not recorded to rest on dusty shelves. God designed them to live in the experiences of people. In preparing this series, the authors never intended merely to increase your intellectual knowledge of the Bible—but to help you put into action the tremendous resources available in Jesus Christ.

"We'll take some frankincense and myrrh and if you have any gold, we'll take that too!"

1.
Immanuel

Study passage: Luke 2:1-20

Focus: Luke 2:11: Today in the town of David a Savior has been born to you; he is Christ the Lord.

---

1 More than 500 years before Jesus' birth, a prophet named Isaiah told what would happen: "The virgin will be with child and will give birth to a son, and they will call him Immanuel — which means, God with us'" (Matthew 1:23 and Isaiah 7:14).

Begin your personal study by reading Luke 2:1-20 two or three times. First, read it quickly to acquaint yourself with the content. Next, read it slowly and carefully.

2 Identify one significant *action* in each of the following groups of verses.

1-5

Joseph and Mary go to Bethlehem.

6-7

8-12

13-14

15-16

17-18

19-20

The statements that you wrote above form an overview of the birth of Jesus. This kind of exercise will help you

- remember the event.
- identify the most important parts of the event.
- see how the parts relate.

3 Even though He was born in the most humble surroundings, it is clear that Jesus was a unique person. Find the names, titles, and descriptions of Jesus in the following verses:

Verse 7	Verse 11	Verse 12

List any other descriptions of Jesus you found while studying the passage.

Select one name, title, or description of Jesus and tell why it is meaningful to you.

---

4 Imagine you are one of the shepherds gathered around a fire to ward off the night's chill. Suddenly the darkness is shattered by the appearance of an angel — and then a choir of angels. What emotions do you feel when the angels appear?

How did the shepherds respond?

How do you think you would have felt when you heard the message in verses 10-14?

---

5 After they saw and heard the angels, what did the shepherds do? (There are several actions mentioned.)

Why do you think they were so eager to tell others?

Do the same things motivate you to talk about Jesus today? Explain your answer.

If not, what does motivate you to tell others about Him?

6 As you consider this story of the first Christmas, list the facts *you* consider most important. Don't attempt to figure out what others might say. There are no right or wrong answers. This question is designed to help you concentrate on the passage and draw your own conclusions.

Are these facts usually emphasized at Christmas time?

As a result of your study, what ideas do you have to make your celebration of Christmas more meaningful? (You might consider using these ideas to introduce a new family "tradition" in your Christmas celebration.)

7 As you contemplate the Christmas story, you may picture a manger in a stable—humble beginnings for the One the angels called Immanuel, God with you. Jesus took the first step, opening the door to God in you.

What difference does it make to have God in you? You may answer this question from the thoughts in the passage or from the feelings you have when you study it.

O Holy Child of Bethlehem
Descend to us, we pray;
Cast out our sin, and enter in,
Be born in us today.
We hear the Christmas angels
The great glad tidings tell;
O come to us, abide with us,
Our Lord Immanuel!

Phillips Brooks
Hymn

2.
The Word

Study passage: John 1:1-18

Focus: John 1:14: The Word became flesh and lived for a while among us. We have seen his glory, the glory of the one and only Son, who came from the Father, full of grace and truth.

1 Our usual thoughts of the Christmas story bring to mind a picture of Jesus as a baby, tender and helpless. John tells the Christmas story from a different perspective. He presents the Word as having power and authority, and entering history as part of a timeless plan. Instead of telling of shepherds in a field he talks about the Lamb who will remove sin.

Read John 1:1-18 two or three times. List any statements that seem particularly important to *you*.

2 One clue to help you determine what the writer considered important is the repetition of a word, phrase, or concept. *The Word* is used four times in this passage. In verses 1-5, what statements reveal that *the Word* refers to God? If you find other statements in the rest of the study passage, list those also.

In verse 14, what statements reveal that *the Word* refers to Jesus? If you find other statements in the rest of the study passage, list those also.

3 John states, "The Word became flesh" as historic reality with implications for all time and all people. What are some of the benefits you can enjoy because the Word became flesh?

Verse 4

Light is available to me.

Verse 12

Verse 16

Verse 17

Verse 18

4 Perhaps the most important benefit Jesus provided for you is the opportunity to become a child of God. Read verses 10-13. How does a person become a child of God?

How do you know you are a child of God?

5 John the Baptist was appointed by God to pave the way for the coming Messiah (verses 6-9). What did John say about Jesus? See verse 15.

6 John said he was unworthy to untie the thongs of the Messiah's sandals. In what ways have you seen the worthiness of the Word in your study of John 1:1-18?

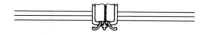

That which was from the beginning, which we have heard, which we have seen with our eyes, which we have looked at and our hands have touched—this we proclaim concerning the Word of life. The life appeared; we have seen it and testify to it, and we proclaim to you the eternal life, which was with the Father and has appeared to us. We proclaim to you what we have seen and heard, so that you also may have fellowship with us. And our fellowship is with the Father and with his Son, Jesus Christ.

John the Apostle
1 John 1:1-3

"You must be born again."

3.
Savior

Study passage: John 3:1-21

Focus: John 3:16: For God so loved the world that he gave his one and only Son, that whoever believes in him shall not perish but have eternal life.

1 A savior rescues or delivers someone from peril. Jesus is called the Savior because He rescues people from ultimate peril.

Read John 3:1-21 two or three times. As you read, ask God to emphasize a thought from the passage that you can "take with you."

2 The passage relates a conversation between Jesus and a man named Nicodemus. One way to study a conversation is to restate it in an abbreviated form. Working on a shortened version of the conversation will help you examine it closely to determine each main thought.

An abbreviated version of Jesus' conversation with Nicodemus is given below. In each blank, write the verse number where that thought can be found. Not every verse in the passage will be recorded. If you feel the abbreviated conversation below misses some important points, add your changes to the dialogue.

_____ Nicodemus: "Your miracles show that God has sent you."

_____ Jesus: "To see God, you have to be born twice."

_____ Nicodemus: "Physically, that just doesn't make sense."

_____ Jesus: "The second time is a spiritual birth."

_____ Nicodemus: "How can that be done?"

_____ Jesus: "Those who believe, gain eternal life."

3 Clearly, being born again stands out as one of the main topics of the conversation. What does the passage *say* about being born again?

Verse 3

Verse 7

In verses 3-8, what else is implied about being born again?

4 Perhaps because Jesus was talking to a teacher of the Old Testament, He referred to an episode in Israel's history (verse 14). Read the account of this event in Numbers 21:4-9. How is Jesus like the bronze snake?

5 The Israelites were saved from the poisonous snakes, but God has provided more important salvation for you. To understand this salvation, begin by listing some facts found in the study passage.

What is God's attitude toward you? (Verse 16)

What action did He take? (Verse 16)

What response would be appropriate for you? (Verse 16)

What does God promise to those who respond in this way? (Verse 16)

Why did He send His Son? (Verse 17)

What two groups of people are listed in verse 18?

What can be said about a person who is attracted to "light"?
(Verses 19-21)

---

6 Based on your entire study, how would you say a person
becomes born again in the sense that Jesus meant it?

What gives you personal assurance that Jesus is your Savior?

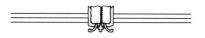

The end of the story . . .

When the Pharisees challenged the validity of
Jesus' ministry, Nicodemus asked them, "Does our
law condemn a man without first hearing him to
find out what he is doing?" (John 7:51).

After Jesus' death, John records, "Nicodemus
brought a mixture of myrrh and aloes, about
seventy-five pounds" to prepare Jesus' body
for burial (John 19:39).

These two incidents offer glimpses of
Nicodemus's response to Jesus and lead
historians to conclude that he had become
a believer in Jesus Christ.

4.
Friend of Sinners

Study passage: John 4:4-26

Focus: John 4:9: The Samaritan woman said to him, "You are a Jew and I am a Samaritan woman. How can you ask me for a drink?" (For Jews do not associate with Samaritans.)

1 Religious leaders viewed Jesus with disdain. "How," they asked, "could He be a leader and be a friend to common and irreligious people?" He was known to eat with dishonest tax collectors, discuss issues with known ne'er-do-wells, and even speak with prostitutes. He was a friend of sinners.

Begin your study by reading the passage several times, asking God to give you one thought to meditate on during the week.

2 This passage is similar to the passage in chapter 3 because it records a conversation between Jesus and another person. The beginning of the conversation has been restated to emphasize the main ideas. Complete the conversation by restating the main idea in the remaining verses.

Jesus:
Verses 7-8

Please give me some water.

Woman:
Verse 9

Why do you ask me?

Jesus:
Verse 10

If you understood, you would ask for living water.

Woman:
Verses 11-12

Jesus:
Verses 13-14

Woman:
Verse 15

Jesus:
Verse 16

Woman:
Verse 17

Jesus:
Verses 17-18

Woman:
Verses 19-20

Jesus:
Verses 21-24

Woman:
Verse 25

Jesus:
Verse 26

3 The two people with whom Jesus talked were extremely different. List the differences you see between Nicodemus and the woman at the well.

Nicodemus	Woman at the well

In what ways do you identify with Nicodemus?

In what ways do you identify with the woman?

What does Jesus' ability to relate to both of these people imply about His ability to relate to you?

4 When the woman expressed concern about the correct location for worship, she referred to differing opinions between the Samaritans and Jews. The Samaritans considered Mount Gerizim to be the sacred place. According to their tradition, it was there that Abraham prepared to offer Isaac as a sacrifice. The Jews considered Jerusalem and the temple there to be the proper location for worship. But Jesus pointed out that other issues were more important.

According to verses 20-25, what is not important for worship?

What is important for worship?

What in your weekly worship service helps you emphasize the important issues of worship?

5 Look again at verses 13 and 14. What do you think Jesus meant by the term *living water*?

In what sense have you "drunk" this water?

How has it kept you from becoming "thirsty" again?

---

6 The incident in this passage took place between a Jew (Jesus) and a Samaritan (the woman). At the time of this meeting, more than 700 years of racial and religious prejudice existed between the two races. The Jews hated this mixed race of Jews and foreigners, and avoided traveling through their country.

Jesus chose to go through Samaria. What did He do to communicate acceptance to this woman?

How can you follow His example and communicate acceptance to people with whom you do not normally associate?

This man welcomes sinners and eats with them.

The Pharisees speaking of Jesus
Luke 15:2

5.
Master

Study passage: Matthew 8:23–9:8

Focus: Matthew 8:27: The men were amazed and asked, "What kind of man is this? Even the winds and the waves obey him!"

1 The people who called Jesus "Master" were expressing their allegiance to Him and to His teachings. They also knew there was no obstacle He could not overcome.

Begin your study by reading the passage several times. Briefly record some of the blessings you receive.

2 In the study passage, Jesus demonstrates His mastery in three situations. Complete the chart below.

Briefly describe the miracle.	What kind of authority does this demonstrate?
Matthew 8:23-27 *Jesus stops the storm.*	
Matthew 8:28-34	*He has power over evil beings.*
Matthew 9:1-8	

3 Although the demons would not submit to Jesus, their response shows that they knew He was Master. Read what the demons said in verses 29-31. What does that indicate about who Jesus is (His position)?

What does that indicate about what He can do (His authority)?

4 Jesus said that He healed a paralytic to show that He also had power to forgive sins. How do you think this miracle showed He had authority to forgive?

5 The observers responded in a different way to each of the miracles Jesus performed. Write a short phrase to describe each response.

8:27

8:34

9:8

Today also, many people will respond to Jesus in one of these three ways. Choose one response listed above. How would you help someone who has responded in this way to make Jesus the Master of his or her life?

6 What evidence in these three events shows that Jesus is, in fact, Lord and Master?

7 This Scripture passage shows Jesus exercising His mastery over nature, spiritual beings, and physical bodies. How does the authority of Jesus affect the way you live today?

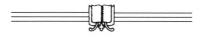

A prayer for you to finish . . .

Lord, You truly are Master—of nature, of spiritual and physical things. I want You to be my Master—of my attitudes, my decisions, my . . .

6.
Christ

Study passage: Matthew 16:13-28

Fc cus: Matthew 16:16: Simon Peter answered, "You are the Christ, the Son of the living God."

1 The word *Christ* literally means "anointed of God." For centuries the Jews anticipated God's Anointed One coming to free God's people from political tyranny and oppression. Jesus, the Christ, did come to lead God's people and to deliver them from oppression, but not in the way the Jews expected.

Read the study passage several times, using different translations. If questions come to your mind as you read, jot them down. Some of your questions will be answered as you complete this chapter study. Some may be resolved through discussion with others. And some may remain unanswered.

---

2 A clear understanding of Jesus' identity is necessary to relate to Him properly. What were some of the wrong ideas people had about who Jesus was?

What are some other misconceptions people have about Jesus today?

---

3 One of the clearest statements about the identity of Jesus was given by Peter in this passage. Yet a later conversation showed that Peter lacked full understanding of Jesus. Use the chart below to note the differences in Jesus' two conversations with Peter.

Verses 13-19	Verses 21-23
The topic of conversation	
Peter's comment to Jesus	
Jesus' response to Peter	

4 Understanding verses 24-28 will shed light on Jesus' second conversation with Peter. What does Jesus say about the person who wants to save his life?

What does Jesus say about the person who loses his life for Him?

Refer to your chart in question 3. Was Peter trying to help Jesus save His life or lose His life?

Was Jesus helping Peter to save his life or lose his life? Explain.

5 Losing your life for Jesus includes following Him. In verse 24, Jesus gives instructions for a person who wishes to follow Him.

What I should do	How I can do this

According to the study passage, why is it reasonable to do these things?

What other reasons to do these things would you give?

6 In response to the great confession of Peter ("You are the Christ, the Son of the living God"), Jesus speaks about the Church: "The gates of Hades will not overcome it." What does His statement indicate about the character of His Church?

How do the ministries of your church provide evidence of one characteristic you listed?

Today, equipped with the New Testament, churches, preachers, and Christian books and schools, it is easier to answer Jesus' question, "Who do you say I am?" Yet, His question is not trivial. Imagine that Jesus asks you, "Who do you say I am?" What will your response be?

WHO DO YOU SAY I AM?

35

"Very funny, very funny."

7.
Servant

Study passage: John 13:1-17

Focus: John 13:14-15: Now that I, your Lord and Teacher, have washed your feet, you also should wash one another's feet. I have set you an example that you should do as I have done for you.

1 To many people, the title of "servant" indicates a position of inferiority. Jesus showed that serving was an action of the highest order. He elevated the concept of serving to a position of dignity and value.

Footwashing was a hospitable service offered to house guests. The servant usually performed this task, but the host might wash the feet of special guests.

Read this passage several times. The last time, read it slowly and thoughtfully. Imagine yourself among Jesus and the disciples. Jesus stands up, takes the position of a servant, and begins washing your feet. Record the feelings you might have as this takes place.

2 When a passage contains both conversation and actions, it is usually best to consider the actions first. This will often give you insight into what is said. What actions take place in the study passage?

Verse(s)	Action

3 A person's actions often indicate what he is thinking. According to verses 1-3, of what was Jesus aware?

Verse 1

Verse 2

Verse 3

How do you think this awareness affected His actions?

4 Jesus washed the disciples' feet and said, "You also should wash one another's feet" (verse 14). What attitudes did Jesus reveal in His example?

What opportunities for service in your church allow you to express the same attitudes as Jesus did?

5 What other titles and descriptions of Jesus, besides servant, are stated or implied in this passage?

Verse	Title or description	Would this person usually serve or be served?
1		
3		
6		
13		
16		
Others you might find		

As you review your answers to this chart, what conclusions do you draw?

6 You began this chapter by focusing on the actions of Jesus, with the expectation that they would help you understand His comments. What do you consider to be the most important thing(s) that He said in this passage? Why?

7 What service can you perform this week to gain the blessing promised in verse 17?

On a speaking trip through Asia, a Christian leader was accompanied everywhere by his interpreter. They often traveled along very muddy roads and trails. At the conclusion of the trip, someone asked the interpreter, "After hearing so many messages by this Christian leader, what impressed you the most?"
Replied the interpreter, "He shined my shoes."[1]

Note
1. Adapted from *True Fellowship*, by Jerry Bridges (Colorado Springs, Colorado: NavPress, 1985), page 167.

8.
Bread of Life

Study passage: Mark 14:12-42

Focus: Mark 14:22: While they were eating, Jesus took bread, gave thanks and broke it, and gave it to his disciples, saying, "Take it; this is my body."

1 When God gave the Israelites manna to eat in the wilderness, they called it bread from Heaven. But the greatest Bread from Heaven came years later.

Read Mark 14:12-42 daily. Imagine you are reclining at the table with Jesus. Picture what the room looks like. What is said before and after Jesus' statements? Think about other details related to this event.

2 When Jesus first declared, "I am the bread of life" (John 6:35), many of His followers were confused. They also heard Him say, "Whoever eats my flesh and drinks my blood has eternal life" (John 6:54). Today, through the observance of Communion, people everywhere remember how Jesus is their Bread of Life.

To gain a perspective of the events surrounding the Last Supper (the first Communion), briefly describe what is happening in each group of verses below.

Verses 12-16

Verses 17-21

Verses 22-26

Verses 27-31

Verses 32-36

Verses 37-42

3 The Passover was an annual remembrance of how the Jewish people were freed from slavery in Egypt. God sent a series of plagues on the Egyptian people to force them to free the Jews.

The final plague was to send the death angel to kill the oldest son in every home. The faithful Jews were told by Moses to sacrifice a lamb and put its blood on the doorposts of their homes. Then the death angel would *pass over* them.

Thus, it was called the Passover, one of the most important holy days for Jews. They celebrated this event by sacrificing a lamb and eating a special meal that recreated their last supper in Egypt.

What similarities do you see between the Passover and this occasion of Christ's impending death?

4 Jesus gave the Passover meal a new significance. The broken bread helps us remember the physical suffering Jesus endured for us. The wine helps us remember His blood poured out for our sins. Today we remember this event through Communion.

People have described Communion in various ways. In what ways do you see it

as worship?

as a celebration?

as a means of grace?

5 After the Passover supper, Jesus led the disciples to Gethsemane for a time of prayer. How did Jesus feel?

Study Jesus' prayer in this passage. What do you think was His view . . .

of God?	of Himself?	of His circumstances?

6 After eating the meal, Jesus said one of the disciples would betray Him. Later that evening, He told them they would "fall away" (deny knowing Him). As He prayed in Gethsemane, the disciples fell asleep. What do you consider to be parallel actions for these things today?

Betrayal

Falling away

Falling asleep

7 Though the disciples did deny Jesus and did fall asleep, they also demonstrated several good qualities. Read through the passage and list those qualities.

8 When Jesus called the bread of the passover His "body," He was emphasizing that He is the Bread of Life. Thinking of this week's study and other Scripture, how is Jesus like bread?

How do you expect your understanding of Jesus as the Bread of Life to enhance your communion observances and your communion with Christ as a way of life?

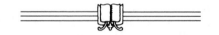

For I received from the Lord what I also passed on to you: The Lord Jesus, on the night he was betrayed, took bread, and when he had given thanks, he broke it and said, "This is my body, which is for you; do this in remembrance of me." In the same way, after supper he took the cup, saying, "This cup is the new covenant in my blood; do this, whenever you drink it, in remembrance of me." For whenever you eat this bread and drink this cup, you proclaim the Lord's death until he comes.

Paul
1 Corinthians 11:23-26

"... and for Jim and Betty, as they ..."

9.
Great High Priest

Study passage: John 17

Focus: John 17:17-19: Sanctify them by the truth; your word is truth. As you sent me into the world, I have sent them into the world. For them I sanctify myself, that they too may be truly sanctified.

1 Under God's old covenant with Israel, the priests represented the people to God by offering sacrifices and prayers on their behalf. Under the new covenant, Jesus is your priest. He prayed for you and sacrificed His life when He was on earth, and He prays for you now.

Read John 17 several times. The final time, read the chapter aloud, substituting your name for the pronouns *they, them*, etc. How does this make you feel?

2 When completed, the following chart will give you a short survey of the people and requests in Jesus' prayer.

Who He prayed for	What He prayed
Verse 1	Verse 1
	Verse 2
	Verse 5
Verse 9	Verse 11
	Verse 15
	Verse 17
Verse 20	Verse 21
	Verse 23
	Verse 24

Who did Jesus not pray for? (Verse 9)

3 Considering what you have learned in the first two questions, what do you conclude were the main things on Jesus' mind?

4 According to verse 4, how did Jesus glorify God?

What other statements in Jesus' prayer support this?

What do you think must be true for a person to be able to make the same statement as Jesus did in verse 4?

5 Part of Jesus' work was to relate correctly to His society. You should, too. What does this prayer indicate your relationship to your community should be? See verses 13-18. (You may find other relevant material in the rest of the study passage.)

6 Your relationship to other believers should have a different quality from your relationship to your community. Jesus made a strong plea for unity of His followers. In your church, what can promote the kind of oneness Jesus desires?

Explain why unity, or oneness, does not mean you have to forsake your personality and ideas.

7 Jesus Christ is the Great High Priest. And according to 1 Peter 2:9, "you . . . are a royal priesthood." As a priest, you have access to God. You can go to Him on behalf of others.

Review all you've learned in studying this passage. If you were to copy the example of Jesus' prayer, for whom would you pray and what would you pray for them?

Who	What

8 Jesus said that He sanctified Himself for the sake of His followers. To sanctify means to set apart for service to God. In the Old Testament, the priests were sanctified in the sense that they were exempt from many responsibilities so they could perform their duties. They also performed rituals of sanctification that included special observances, sacrifices, and offerings.

What did Jesus say about your sanctification in His prayer?

What does it mean to you to know you are set apart for God's service (sanctified)?

What responsibility do you think you have to sanctify yourself?

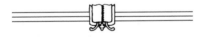

Such a high priest meets our need—one who is holy, blameless, pure, set apart from sinners, exalted above the heavens.

Author of Hebrews
Hebrews 7:26

10.
Man of Sorrows

Study passage: John 19:16-30

Focus: John 19:30: When he had received the drink, Jesus said, "It is finished." With that, he bowed his head and gave up his spirit.

---

1 It was a dark day, literally, figuratively, and spiritually. The One who desired to do nothing but to give, to help, to enlighten was arrested, tortured, and executed in the most brutal way. Deprived of dignity and friends, forsaken by God, He was truly the Man of Sorrows.

Read the study passage several times, using different translations to aid your understanding.

The Trial and Execution of Jesus	
(Taken from the four Gospels)	
APPROXIMATE TIME	ACTIVITY
Late evening	He prays in Gethsemane.
Midnight	He is betrayed and arrested. Friends forsake Him.
1:00 a.m.	He stands before Annas. The officers hit Him.
2:00–5:00 a.m.	He is taken to Caiaphas, the high priest. He stands before the whole Council, and several false witnesses testify. They find Him worthy of death. Several men spit on Him, then slap Him and beat Him.
6:00–7:00 a.m.	The Council plots to execute Jesus and takes Him to Pilate. Pilate sends Him to Herod to stand trial. Herod finds Him innocent but sends Him back to Pilate, who condemns Him to death.
8:00 a.m.	He is whipped with a "scourge." A "crown" of thorns is put on His head while the soldiers spit on Him and hit Him in the face and head with bamboo-like rods.
10:00 a.m.	They take Him to Golgotha and nail Him to a cross. He hangs there to die.
3:00 p.m.	Jesus cries out, "My God, my God, why have you forsaken me?" He says, "It is finished," and dies.

2 Thinking of the above summary, what do you consider to be one of the most painful things Jesus endured? Why?

3 Jesus did not die in vain. He deliberately submitted to death. Using the study passage and other Scripture, explain that Jesus' death was not merely a cruel twist of fate.

4 Complete one of the exercises below.

a. Briefly tell what Jesus accomplished on the Cross according to the following references:

Romans 5:10

Colossians 1:20

Hebrews 2:14-15

b. Find at least two Bible references that tell what Jesus accomplished on the Cross. You may want to consult a concordance. Look up verses listed under the words cross, death, or blood. Not every reference you find will be helpful, but you will find some possibilities.

5 One evidence that Jesus' death was part of God's eternal plan is the repeated prophecies about it. Isaiah foretold the death of Jesus about 700 years before it happened. List at least three ways Jesus' death is described in Isaiah 53.

6 Consider what you've learned about the Man of Sorrows—the prophecy of His death, the pain, and the purpose. Then explain what meaning you give to His last words, "It is finished." Remember, with this kind of question, there are many answers.

"Man of Sorrows," what a name
For the son of God who came
Ruined sinners to reclaim!
Hallelujah! what a Savior!

Bearing shame and scoffing rude,
In my place condemned He stood;
Sealed my pardon with His blood;
Hallelujah! what a Savior!

Lifted up was He to die,
"It is finished," was His cry;
Now in heav'n exalted high;
Hallelujah! what a Savior!

Philip P. Bliss
Hymm

"I wonder what this will do to our pension plan!"

11.
Lord God Omnipotent

Study passage: Luke 24

Focus: Luke 24:5-6: In their fright the women bowed down with their faces to the ground, but the men said to them, "Why do you look for the living among the dead? He is not here; he has risen!"

1 The sorrow of Jesus' death was not final. Jesus chose not to remain dead. He showed His unequaled power by returning to life. He is Lord over death. He reigns over all. He is Lord God Omnipotent.

Read the chapter several times, the first time early in the week. Day by day keep foremost in your mind the fact that

Jesus rose from the dead. As you do so, record any differences in your attitudes and actions.

2 Some people claim that Jesus rose only spiritually, not literally. What evidence in the passage shows that Jesus had a physical body after His resurrection?

3 Many people were reluctant to accept the fact of Jesus' return from death. But those who saw Him were convinced beyond doubt.

Complete the chart below based on what is stated or implied in the passage.

What convinced them	How they reacted
The women (verses 1-11)	
The two men (verses 13-35)	
The eleven (verses 36-53)	

When you became convinced that Jesus had risen from the dead, how did your reaction compare to the ones above?

4 The conviction these people had that Jesus was alive undoubtedly grew deeper as they continued to see and hear Him for several weeks. Then Jesus commissioned His disciples to proclaim His message. List what you learn in verses 44-49 about

Jesus.

His message.

the messengers.

how this commission applies to you.

5 One way to prepare yourself to convey the gospel to others is to be ready to show them that Jesus has risen. What evidence could *you* offer that the story of His resurrection is not a myth? In addition to the scriptural record, you might include other historical evidence, logic, what other people have said, and your personal experience and testimony.

6 In the previous chapter, you examined what Jesus accomplished through His death. Now, examine what He accomplished through His resurrection. Complete one of the two exercises below.

a. Briefly tell what Jesus accomplished through His resurrection according to the following verses:

Romans 4:25

1 Corinthians 15:20-22

1 Peter 1:3-4

b. Find at least two other references that show the importance of Jesus' resurrection and state briefly what they teach. If you do not know where to find verses like this, look in a concordance under the words rose, risen, or resurrection.

7 When Jesus rose from the dead, He showed that He was Lord God Omnipotent. What to you are some other important aspects of the Resurrection?

He is risen. Hallelujah!

"Our bylaws specifically state that the will of God cannot be overturned without a ⅔ majority vote."

12.
King of Kings

Study passage: Acts 1:1-11

Focus: Acts 1:11: "Men of Galilee," they said, "why do you stand here looking into the sky? This same Jesus, who has been taken from you into heaven, will come back in the same way you have seen him go into heaven."

1 Jesus rose. He defeated death. It could never trouble Him again. He was victorious, and now He was ready to take His position on the throne over all other thrones and powers. He was ready to rule as the King over all other kings.

Read Acts 1:1-11 several times. The event recorded in this

passage is usually referred to as the Ascension. Briefly
describe what happened.

2 After the Resurrection, Jesus remained on earth for forty
days. What did He do during this period?

Acts 1:3

1 Corinthians 15:3-7

3 Jesus couldn't die again. If He had not ascended, He
would still be walking on earth. What do you think He
could be accomplishing if He were still on earth?

According to the study passage, what things has Jesus
accomplished through His ascension?

Why is it important to you that Jesus ascended?

61

4 Before He ascended, Jesus told the eleven remaining disciples that they would be His witnesses (Acts 1:8). To understand this statement, begin by checking a dictionary definition of the word *witness*. Briefly state it.

In what way were the eleven to be witnesses?

Though you did not see Jesus crucified and raised, in what sense do you think you *are* a witness for Him?

5 In verse 8, Jesus told His disciples their outreach would affect people through ever-increasing spheres of influence. Identify these spheres on the diagram below.

Jerusalem

What are your comparable spheres of influence?

Your first area of influence is the people near you now. Give a brief description of what you are doing or can do

- to improve your relationship with these people in order to open doors of communication.

- to prepare yourself to explain the gospel to them.

6 Jesus was not going to leave the disciples alone in their task of being witnesses. He would soon send the Holy Spirit. What did Jesus teach in Acts 1:1-11 about the Holy Spirit?

7 When Jesus ascended, He took His rightful place at the right hand of God. In time, He will return in power as the King of kings. What is revealed in the study passage about His return?

What makes you eager for the return of the Lord?

Jesus is a King unlike other kings. He does not rule with pomp and ceremony, but in humility and grace. You've studied the eternal Word born in a stable. The Christ and Master is not aloof and distant, but a Savior who is a friend and servant. At times—beaten, tortured, crucified—He did not seem to be the King at all. But the Lord of all could not be held by death; He rose triumphantly.

After Jesus proved His claim of lordship by rising from the dead, He lived on earth forty days. This allowed hundreds of people to see and hear Him and to testify to others of His resurrection. He ascended to Heaven so He could send the Holy Spirit to all who believe. Someday He will return and assume His rightful place above all creation as the King of kings.

Developing Lifelong Study Skills

The variety of methods you followed to complete the study are skills you can use throughout your life to understand and apply other passages in the Bible.

This summary identifies a few of the skills covered in this book, and will serve as a helpful guide for your future Bible study.

1. ACTION OVERVIEW. In chapter 1, question 2, you listed the main actions in the passage. This allows you to see the thrust of a passage and how the verses relate to one another. This method is used primarily when studying a narrative. Although they appeared in a different form, action overviews were also used in chapter 7, question 2 (a chart) and chapter 8, question 2.

2. RESTATEMENT. In chapters 3 and 4, you related in your own words the conversations Jesus had with Nicodemus and the woman at the well. This required you to first understand what was being said. This understanding is the primary value of any restatement. You can use this method profitably for virtually any passage.

3. QUESTIONING. You studied John 3:16 and the following verses by answering a series of short questions (chapter 3, question 5). Although the questions were not particularly difficult, they helped clarify the content of the passage. When you study a passage independently, you need to develop your own list of questions. Using short, direct questions will often help you correct initial wrong impressions.

4. PERSONALIZATION. While studying the prayer of Jesus (chapter 9, question 1), you were instructed to refer to yourself as you repeated the prayer. This process helps you see how a teaching affects your life. For many people, there is a significant difference between saying, "God forgives sinners" and "God has forgiven me."

5. VISUALIZATION. In chapters 1 and 7, you were asked to imagine the scriptural setting. As you visualize something, you will often picture details and even feel emotions that can cause the event to come alive for you.